Everything Is Temporary

Everything Is Temporary

Small Impulses for an easier Life

Mario Lopez

IMPRINT

Everything Is Temporary
Small Impulses for an easier Life
Original title: *Alles ist temporär*

Author: Mario Lopez
Published by: ML Publishing
Margarethenstr. 7
47226 Duisburg, Germany

Website: www.ml-publishing.com
Email: book@ml-publishing.com

Publisher's note: This book includes, among other things, the author's personal experiences and reflections.

First edition: 2026
ISBN: 978-3-912373-15-8
Cover design: Mico Lopez
Editing: Mico Lopez

TABLE OF CONTENTS

A Few Words Up Front

This book is for you.

It's about things that can happen to all of us: loss, pain, fear, but also hope, new beginnings, and those small moments that help us stand back up.

I'm not writing to sound clever. I'm writing because I've lived through how fast everything can change. You think you have things under control, and then life comes along and shows you something else.

The most important thought in this book is simple: everything is temporary. What's weighing on you right now won't last forever. What scares you won't hang over you for eternity. And even sadness doesn't get the final word. It won't stay the way it is — and that can help us keep going.

But this isn't only true for hard times. The good doesn't last forever either. Beautiful moments pass. Happiness comes and goes. And that's exactly why we shouldn't overlook those moments, postpone them, or tell ourselves we'll make up for them "someday." If things are good right now, enjoy it. Breathe it in. Be here. Because this moment will pass too.

Read this book slowly, maybe just one chapter a day, take what fits you, and if a sentence makes you pause for a second, then that's exactly right.

I hope you find something in these pages that lets you breathe a little easier.

Introduction

Everything is temporary. Three simple words, and yet they hold more truth than many of us want to admit. Nothing stays the way it is. Not pain. Not joy. Not even life itself. Everything changes, and in that change there's meaning, too.

This book isn't a guide telling you how to live. It's more like a companion: honest, simple, and human. It holds thoughts and experiences from a real life. Some were beautiful, others were painful, but they all had one thing in common: they showed me that even things that seem endless will pass.

I didn't write this because I have everything figured out. I wrote it because life teaches us, sometimes gently, sometimes the hard way. People come and go. Times change. Even the moments that shape us the most don't stay forever.

So who is this book for? For anyone who thinks too much sometimes. For those who take life too serious. For people who worry, who doubt, and don't always know where to put their thoughts. For anyone who wants to learn to let go, to experience the present more consciously. And also for those going through a hard time right now, and maybe just need something small to hold on to.

In life, we often try to hold on: to people, to success, to moments. But everything has its season, and sometimes you only realize that when something is already gone. Life teaches patience. And it reminds us again and again that nothing lasts forever, not the good, and not the bad.

As you read this book, I hope you pause every now and then. I hope you see that even difficult phases pass, and that you learn to enjoy the beautiful moments more consciously. Because every moment, no matter how small, is unique and can never be repeated.

And maybe this book will help you take things a little more lightly. Because in the end, the truth remains the same:

Everything is temporary.

The Oldest Proof?

When you think about the word "temporary," you often think about your own life first. Change. Getting older. A beginning and an end.

But what happens when you widen your view, much wider. So far that you can see the bigger picture.

Scientists assume that everything began around 13.8 billion years ago with the Big Bang. A moment that is almost impossible to imagine. Out of what seems like nothing, space and time appeared, energy and matter, and since then the universe has been expanding.

Galaxies form. They move, collide, and change. Stars are born, shine for millions of years, and burn out. Even our sun, the one that gives us light and warmth every day, will one day go out. Not today and not tomorrow, but one day.

Even planets and moons are, in the end, only here for a while. They come into existence, they change, and they disappear again.

If you really take that in, one thing becomes clear: nothing lasts forever, not even the stars. Maybe not even time, at least not the way we understand it today.

Now place this next to this: the average life expectancy worldwide is about 73 years. In many countries it is 80 or a little more. Compared to 13.8 billion years, a human life is almost nothing. In percentage terms, a whole life is about 0.0000005 percent of the universe's existence so far. A dot so small you can barely see it.

And yet we often take our short time here extremely serious. We get upset. We argue. We fight. As if everything will last forever. But we are only visiting for a moment, a tiny stage.

That's why it makes sense to use this time well: live, love, laugh, feel instead of making everything more difficult, especially not for yourself. Because even the biggest worries will one day grow quieter. They fade, like a star whose light still travels toward us for a long time, even though the star itself has been gone for ages.

Maybe that is the oldest proof of all:

Everything is temporary.

Carpe Diem – This Day Is Temporary

Sounds powerful. A lot of people have it on the wall as a slogan. And still, we often live the exact opposite way. The day passes by, we function, and we're already thinking about tomorrow while today hasn't even really started.

Not long ago, we celebrated my son's 19th birthday. Shortly before that, he had moved into his own place for university. I felt proud. I felt happy. And then there was this quiet feeling that slipped in between it all: another chapter is already over.

My two older children were there too. I looked at them and realized: this is one of those moments you can't hold on to, but you can't afford to miss either. A new path is starting for them, and for me as well. The day was beautiful. We laughed, talked, remembered. And that's exactly why it was dangerous, because moments like that pass quickly, without you noticing.

And then it happened. My mind went wandering. One glance out the window, the half-finished garage, and bang, planning, calculating, next steps, materials, time. Then the leased car, next thought: soon I'll need a replacement, contract, deadlines, paperwork.

And suddenly even the little things showed up, the ones you "just need to do quickly." My head was full, and the moment was gone. Something snapped inside me:

Stop. Cut it out.

There you are, in a happy moment, with people who matter to you, and you're not even there. Only your body is. The rest of you is already somewhere else.

Later, Dr. Ramona Lorenz (PD Dr.) shared a thought with me. She comes from educational research and works a lot with relationships, attention, and truly being present shape everyday life.

"One more thought that stayed with me while reading: being consciously present in the moment is often what creates strong relationships with other people. When a child notices you're only physically present, it strains the relationship, and over time you may become distant. I think children sense this especially strongly, but it applies to other people in life too." — Dr. Ramona Lorenz

Why do we do this? Why is it so hard to simply be here? We live in the rearview mirror or in the calendar, in yesterday or tomorrow, and we overlook the only thing that is real:

Now.

I took a deep breath and pulled myself back. Not later. Now. Stay here. Right here. And then it came back, the moment: warmth, laughter, closeness, that feeling that everything is okay, without having to do anything.

Sometimes life is exactly that, an inner signal that says: wake up. Stay here. Because what we live today is already a memory tomorrow, and every memory begins with a lived now.

Use this day, because it's temporary too.

Don’t take it so hard, everything is temporary

We often make life harder than it must be. We get upset about things we can’t change. We cling to worry, anger, or disappointment as if we must hold on to them. But the truth is simple:

Nothing stays.

Everything moves. Today it’s like this, tomorrow it’s different. A fight can feel like a crack that will never close. A mistake can feel like a stamp on your forehead. A disappointment can feel like a pit in your stomach. But it’s not forever. It’s a chapter, and it passes.

Little things can go to our head, a wrong word, a look, a moment that doesn’t quite go to plan. In that instant it feels huge, almost impossible to get over. And later you look back and think: really? That’s where I burned all that energy?

Life gets easier when you can take one step back inside yourself. Not everything that happens must pull you in. Not everything deserves your full attention. Sometimes it takes one breath and one sentence to bring you back:

This will pass too.

Being calm doesn’t mean you don’t care. It means you decide what matters, and a lot of things don’t.

“When you become aware of that, you also gain a tool to steer yourself through the situation. The temporary becomes a guiding compass: what is worth your time and energy and what is not.”
— Dr. Ramona Lorenz

Today a problem feels big. Tomorrow it’s just a story. The day after tomorrow it might even be something you can smile about.

Live life with more ease. Mistakes are normal. As are setbacks. They're not nothing, but they're not the end either. You can learn from them. You can grow through them. And still, the truth remains: don't break yourself over it.

It happened, you take what it taught you, and then you keep moving, like waves: you get shaken for a moment, and then it becomes calm again.

In the end, what matters isn't what knocked you off track for a moment, but that you kept going.

Don't take it so hard, because everything is temporary.

Death

I was six years old when my mother died. She died in a car accident; it happened while she was taking my father to work.

My father worked on the railway as a shunter. That day he came home covered in blood. He survived the crash; she hadn't. A truck had pulled out in front of them.

I still remember the unrest that suddenly entered our lives, and, at the same time, the silence. Neighbors and friends tried to comfort us, they brought chocolate, trying to do something kind for us children. Whether it helped in that moment, I honestly don't know anymore. I think it was simply too much to understand what had happened.

My father suddenly stood there alone, with four children. He did everything he could to keep everyday life going, but the space my mother left behind couldn't be filled by anyone.

I remember evenings when he sat at the kitchen table — quiet, tired, worn out, and still there. He did his best and never let weakness show.

Back then, I couldn't place the loss. I was afraid and didn't know how things would go on. For a child, death is impossible to grasp. You only feel that something is missing — something that will never come back.

If someone had explained to me, in a way a child could understand, "This pain isn't endless. Like everything in life, it's temporary," it might have helped me handle it differently. But nobody says that to you.

Today, many years later, I see that moment as part of my life — as the beginning of something that shaped me. I learned that even the worst thing changes with time. You keep living. You remember. And you learn how to live with memory.

My wife, Silvina, once said something that stayed with me: the pain never fully goes away, but it changes its colors, its shades. That's exactly how I've experienced it.

Even the deepest pain is temporary — like everything in life.

Feel the Pain

Pain is part of life, whether we want it or not. It reaches us in many different forms — physical, emotional, through loss, disappointment, or goodbyes. Sometimes it gives a warning. Sometimes it arrives out of nowhere, knocks us off balance, and makes us believe nothing will ever be the same again.

But pain never stays the same. It changes, like everything in life. In the beginning it is loud, burning, and hard to bear. With time it becomes quieter. It loses its sharp edge. It turns into a memory, and sometimes, out of that memory, even gratitude can grow.

Many people try to avoid pain. They distract themselves, push it away, escape into work or constant noise. But pain needs to be felt, otherwise it stays. It's like a guest who can only leave once you acknowledge them, once you allow it, listen to it, and understand what it's trying to tell you.

Over the course of my life, I've learned that trying to suppress pain often makes it stronger. But if you accept it consciously, if you feel it without letting it swallow you, you become freer with time.

Pain changes us. It shows us what truly matters. What we love. What we need, and what we don't. It forces us to look. And sometimes, that is exactly its purpose.

So the next time you're hurting, when something hits you in a way that shakes you deeply, remember this: you don't have to fight the pain. You're allowed to feel it. Because it won't last forever. It will grow quieter. It will give you new strength. And one day you'll look back and be able to say: I made it through.

Feel the pain, but know this: it's temporary.

Quitting Is Not an Option

Many of my students know this saying of mine: "Quitting is not an option." It hangs on the wall of our school in large Chinese characters, not because it looks cool, but because I mean it.

When I say it in training, it's not to put pressure on anyone. It's a reminder: strength doesn't start in the muscles. It starts in the mind. Quitting isn't automatically weakness, but choosing to keep going builds charachter.

You see it clearly during endurance training, or exercises that feel like they will never end. Some people draw a line in their head. Others take one step further. There are moments where you can see exactly when someone thinks, I can't do this anymore. And that's when this sentence comes up:

"Quitting is not an option."

Often, it's enough. Suddenly the posture changes. Breathing becomes calmer. Strength shows up again, not because the exhaustion disappears, but because the will becomes stronger. That moment, when someone goes beyond themselves, is priceless. Not only in sport, but in life.

Because in the end, it's rarely talent alone that decides. More often it's endurance. How many competitions have been decided in the very last second? Countless. Whether it's a marathon, football, a driving test, an apprenticeship, or university, in the end, the one who doesn't stop is often the one who wins. Success sometimes has something to do with luck, but almost always with the decision to keep going.

Everyday life is no different. In your job, in relationships, or in your own goals, everyone hits limits at some point. Sometimes you fail. Sometimes you doubt yourself. Sometimes you just want to quit. But if you learn to keep moving even then, you become stronger than any setback — because effort, pain, and exhaustion are not forever.

And sometimes "keep going" doesn't mean pushing through at any cost. Sometimes it means stopping for a moment, catching your breath, and starting again. And sometimes you realize the goal was wrong, or it no longer fits your life. Then it's not quitting. It's a smart adjustment, but it's still not giving up.

Sometimes it takes days. Sometimes weeks or months. Sometimes even years. But nothing stays the same forever. What stays is the memory that you didn't give up. That feels like a quiet victory, not loud, not showy, but it stays with you for a long time.

I've lived this principle again and again: in training, in everyday life, while writing my books, and in projects that cost more energy than people see from the outside. And whenever I was close to throwing everything away, this sentence came back:

"Quitting is not an option."

It follows me like a calm teacher. It reminds me that nothing is permanent, not effort, not pain, not doubt. Everything is temporary. But what grows when you keep going can last. And that's why it's worth getting back up again and again. Only those who continue can grow.

As hard as it can be, even this moment is temporary.

My School Years as the Child of a Guest Worker

After my mother died, we moved to Duisburg Hohenbudberg, into a railway workers' housing area. My father worked there as a shunter for the railway.

He was one of many so called "guest workers" who came to Germany in the early 1960s. My two older siblings were born in the south of Spain. I was born in Rheinhausen, today it's Duisburg Rheinhausen.

After primary school, I was supposed to go, as was common back then, to the nearest school: a Hauptschule (lower secondary school in Germany). On the very first day I noticed I was different. Not only in how I looked, but in my name, and especially in the eyes of the others. For many, I was the foreigner. They didn't always say the word out loud, but you felt it: in looks, in recess, in small comments.

I was the only one in my class with a Spanish name: Mario Lopez.

During that time, I had to learn to stand my ground. There were days when words weren't enough, days when you had to defend yourself without big explanations.

All I really wanted was to belong. But that wasn't easy. I remember many afternoons when I walked home thinking, when will school finally be over? Always these battles, this friction, this constant need to be strong. It felt endless.

Today I know: it was a phase, a hard one, but it taught me a lot.

If a teacher had said to me back then, "everything is temporary, this time will pass, let's work out together how you can get through it", it might have made some things easier. But nobody said that. Back then, people didn't talk about things like that.

And that's exactly why I'm writing this book. It's meant to give courage, to keep going, even when it's hard. Because hard times change too. They pass.

Today I see those school years as one of my most important life lessons. They taught me to be strong and to stand up for myself. I learned that acceptance isn't always given. Sometimes you have to earn it, sometimes you even have to fight for it.

And the most important thing: even though it was hard back then, it was only a chapter. A season. One of many phases that were still to come.

Everything is temporary.

This Too Shall Pass

How often do we make life harder for ourselves. We overthink, we doubt, we get scared, and in the end, what we fear most of the time, doesn't even happen.

We go in circles in our own head, put obstacles in our own way, and forget to live.

I think of situations where I got worked up over small things: a missed appointment, a wrong word, a bill that came out of nowhere. In that moment it felt huge, as if everything was about to fall apart. And a few days later it wasn't even important anymore. Then I asked myself: why did I spend so much energy on this?

A lot of worries are like dark clouds. They look threatening, but often they move on without ever turning into real rain. Once you truly understand that, everything becomes easier.

You sometimes hear a number like "96 percent of our worries never happen." Whether it's exactly that number or not, the thought behind it is true: we give some fears far too much space. We feed them with time, energy, and sleepless nights.

We worry about getting sick. We worry the money won't be enough. We fear losing our partner or our job. And, honestly, you have to ask yourself: how often does that really happen?

Not that often. And even if it does, we almost always find a way. Maybe not immediately. Maybe not perfectly. But somehow, life keeps moving.

Today I know this: a lot of what weighs on us today already feels lighter tomorrow. Some things solve themselves over time. And even hard phases don't last forever.

So don't torture yourself with what you can't change. Trust that everything that happens has its time — and that it will pass again. Because no problem, no fear, no worry lasts forever.

Everything is temporary.

The Butcher

When I was fifteen, I started training as a butcher. Back then people still used the old word: *Metzger.* (German) That first day burned itself into my memory as if it happened yesterday.

That morning I stood in the sausage kitchen. In front of me was a big metal tub — like a bathtub on four legs — filled with blood, tripe, and things that were foreign to me back then and honestly should have stayed foreign.

The smell was heavy. Sharp. Almost unbearable.

Carefully I asked if there was some kind of mixer or machine we could use to blend it all. The answer was dry:

"Roll up your sleeves. You use your arms."

One look at the journeyman's face was enough. That wasn't a joke. He meant it. So I started.

The warm, slippery mess crawled up my forearms. I almost felt sick. But I stayed there — not to look tough, but because I didn't want to disappoint my father. He was raising four children on his own. There was no room for excuses.

The workshop was cold. The work was hard. The pay was small. But the team was good. We laughed together, and that, more than anything, often kept me going.

Over time, routine came: handling the knife, handling the pressure, handling the smells — and handling days that simply aren't pleasant. Discipline wasn't theory. It became daily life.

There was no pocket money, so I had to earn my own. Quitting wasn't an option, so I pushed through.

Back then, it wasn't clear to me what it was all for. Today it is. Those years helped me stand my ground later in life. The training was hard, yes — but it shaped me. Looking back, it wasn't just work. It was growth. It took effort, but it mattered.

And like everything in life, that passed too: the stench, the cold, the exhaustion, the endless days.

My younger brother still teases me about it to this day. He'll grin and say, "Those were the only years you really worked." Then we laugh — and it's clear: that time is long gone.

Everything is temporary.

The Illusion of Control

As humans, we want to have everything under control. We plan, organize, think ahead — hoping it will make us feel safe. But if we're honest, we rarely truly have control in our hands.

We believe we can steer life. But often, life is the one steering us. We make plans, and life makes its own. And sometimes everything turns out differently than we imagined — and that's exactly what unsettles us.

I remember many situations where I thought, everything is going great — and then something happened that I didn't see coming. An unexpected event. A turn. A moment that forced me to let go, to fall, to get back up, and to keep going.

Maybe that's the lesson: control is an illusion. We can control our behavior, but not the outcome. We can prepare and plan — but life always has the final word.

I sometimes think of people who put themselves under pressure because they believe everything has to go perfectly. They cling to plans, ideas, routines — and when something goes wrong, they feel as if they failed. But they didn't fail. They simply forgot that you can't force life.

I've had moments too where I tried to hold on to things that were already gone: relationships, ideas, projects that simply no longer worked. I wanted to save them, fix them, because I believed I could influence the outcome. But at some point I had to let go — and I now believe it was also the best thing for the other person involved.

Today I know this: sometimes the best things happen when you stop fighting. When you accept that life has its own plan. Control matters up to a point — and after that, what you need is trust.

Because even this feeling — that you have to have everything under control — is just a phase. An illusion that passes.

Like everything does. Because everything is temporary.

The Snack Van

After my butcher's apprenticeship, I wanted to build something of my own. I was young, motivated, full of ideas. So I took out a loan with my local bank, and shortly after that it was standing there: a Snack van. That was my first step into self employment.

At nineteen, the van stood in Friemersheim, a district of Duisburg, on the market square. Fries, bratwurst, currywurst, gyros — anything quick that people liked. The van was simple, but I was proud of it. For the first time I had this feeling: now I'm standing on my own feet. Now nobody else decides for me.

We opened in winter — an ice cold November. Some days it was minus twenty degrees. In the morning I stood in the van, my breath visible, my fingers half frozen, and outside hardly anyone wanted to stand there and eat in that weather.

Still, I kept going — with joy — even though the start was tough. And honestly: it got better.

Over time, regular customers came. Many faces became familiar. People liked the food and they liked the way we treated each other — a casual joke, a coffee on the house. That contact with people felt good, and the feeling of having built something felt even better.

But as so often in life, things turned out differently.

One morning there was a letter from the city in my mailbox: "Your van does not fit into the cityscape." Black on white. Hard to believe. Shortly after that, my permit was gone.

Disappointment. Anger. Not knowing what to do. I gave everything — and suddenly it was over.

At the same time, the next news arrived: my first steady girlfriend was pregnant. Nineteen and seventeen. The timing was anything but ideal. I had just started my business, and still one thing was clear: quitting is not an option. Now I needed a secure income.

So I let the snack van go — with a heavy heart. After that, I went back to work as a journeyman in a butcher shop in Duisburg Meiderich, at a company called Massa. It was a step back — and at the same time, a step forward.

Today, when I think of that time, I smile. It taught me a lot: responsibility, courage, and also that setbacks are part of the deal. Nothing stays the same. Sometimes that hurts, and sometimes it's exactly right.

That first business was temporary — but it made me stronger. And that's okay.

Because everything is temporary.

Loss and Gain

In life, you lose a lot: people, things, chances, dreams. And still, with every loss, space opens up — space for something new.

Often you only see that later, when you look back and realize: that cut had to happen so that something else could even become possible.

In my life, there has been more than one moment that felt like an ending. Back then there was pride, motivation, that feeling of finally standing on my own feet.

When I had to give up the snack van, the disappointment was huge. It felt unfair. The future was scary. And in my head there was only one thought: the dream is over.

Today it's clear: it wasn't the end. It was a chapter that had to close so a new one could begin.

Later came the next attempt — self employment again, this time a VHS video rental business. I bought equipment and films, delivered them personally to customers. It went well — until devices broke and some customers simply disappeared with the tapes.

Another setback. Another loss. And then you can only think one thing: I failed again.

With distance, it looks different. I gained more than I could see at the time: responsibility, a better sense for customers, experience in dealing with people — and above all, the ability not to stay down after disappointment.

Getting back up after falling makes you stronger. Not overnight, but step by step.

Losing hurts, yes. But without loss, there is no change. Every step forward means leaving something behind. And sometimes the very thing you lose is the thing that was holding you in place.

When I look back today, one thing becomes clear: every loss created growth. Not because I planned it — but because life demanded it.

Because every loss also carries a gain.

Everything is temporary.

My first Marriage

I met her at fifteen, she was thirteen. We were young, in love, and thought we would be together forever, but life scarily thinks in "forever".

When the message came that she was pregnant, everything changed. Nonetheless it was clear: we would have this child.

As a catholic in the 80s it was hardly imaginable to raise a child illegitimate. So, we decided to marry. She was four months pregnant, and for me it felt like I was old enough to take responsibility.

The day in the hospital is still present to this day. Thirteen hours in the delivery room, exhausted, but filled with pride, then he was there, my son, und suddenly it was clear: I am a father now.

As beautiful as this moment was, as hard was the time that came afterwards. We were young, inexperienced, und the responsibility was bigger than we could understand.

We wanted to be good parents. We loved our child. And then, four months after the birth, came the next announcement: "I'm pregnant again".

Speechless, scared, overwhelmed, doubt, I was everything at once.

An abortion was once again not in the cards. So, we decided to have a second child. It was supposed to be a girl. We wanted to be strong and do the right thing, but the reality was different, harder: two children, little money, high pressure and more fights between two young and obviously overwhelmed parents.

The marriage began to crumble. We would fight often, too often, even in front of the children. I still feel sorry about that to this day.

At some point I decided to move out, not because there was no love, but because it was there, and I did not want the children to suffer under our conflicts. It was a difficult decision but sometimes space apart is the only way to make peace.

Our daughter was born two years before the divorce, a wonderful young girl, to whom I still have an unbreakable bond.

With my son it was often more difficult. It swung between great pride and the thought: Why is he doing this? I believe he never really forgave me for leaving. Nonetheless, the love is there, and we have regular contact. This makes me really happy.

When I look back, I only see mistakes, but I also see lessons. At 21 I already had two children and felt like I had two lives behind me. From present view I was too young for all of that.

It was a time filled with turbulence, but also full of life. It taught me that love is not enough, that responsibility weighs heavy on your shoulders, and that sometimes you need to let go as to not to drown.

That marriage, as short as it was, was a formative chapter.

Everything is temporary.

An Experience That Changed Everything

As a teenager, I was often angry — at everything and everyone. Easily irritated. Quick to explode. Always feeling like I was being treated unfairly.

My circle of friends matched that: loud, hot headed, impulsive. Little money, no plan. And when you're young, you don't think about tomorrow. You just look for some way to get by.

Then something happened that later opened my eyes. I ended up in court — because of assault.

The punishment was community service: paving stones at the Johanniter Hospital, in an ice cold February. That time changed everything.

I still remember those frozen stones. My hands red from the cold. No familiar face around me. No distraction. Just work and time. Time to think. Time to regret. Time to understand.

And one night, a vow formed inside me:

Never again. Never again a situation like this. Never again a mistake like that. Never again that kind of stupidity.

After that experience, I wasn't the same. Something had shifted. Being angry suddenly wasn't "cool" anymore. Anger was just stupid. I wanted things to go differently — for me, for my father, for my family.

Thankfully, the old friends also found their way later on. Work, push through, no more stupid ideas — not because life suddenly became easy, but because it became clear where the wrong path leads.

That one experience taught me more than any book or teacher. It showed how quickly you can slip — and that in the end, only one person decides whether you stay there or change course.

Today it's clear: sometimes you need a shock to wake up. And as terrible as that time felt, in the end it saved me.

Anything that hurts can be a lesson.

And that, too, was temporary.

The VHS Video Rental Service

Before TikTok, X, Facebook, YouTube, Instagram, Netflix, or AI tools, there were VHS tapes — big black plastic cassettes that you slid into a video recorder to watch a movie.

On TV there were three channels: ARD, ZDF, and WDR. If you were lucky, you got a fourth. If you wanted more choice, you went to the video store and rented films.

Video recorders were expensive. Renting was a bit of a hassle — ID, membership card, like a library. And if you returned a tape late, you paid extra fees. Sometimes the penalty was more expensive than the tape itself.

Back then, an idea came up: why not deliver movies straight to people's homes — and bring the video recorder with them?

That's how a small delivery service for films was born.

Maybe it was an early version of Just eat. Just kidding. But I can't help smiling a little as I write that.

I took out a loan, bought five video recorders, and added a selection of popular movies. Small ads ran in local papers.

In the evenings, after my day job, I got started. A suitcase in my hand, the machine under my arm. Customers called on a rotary phone to make an appointment — mobile phones didn't exist yet.

At first, it worked surprisingly well. People loved the idea of watching movies without leaving the house.

Then the problems came. Some machines broke. Some customers moved away and simply kept the tapes — or the recorder. Others suddenly stopped opening the door, or didn't answer the phone anymore.

After a few months, it was clear: this model wouldn't last long. Money lost again. Time invested again. And again, something learned. Being self employed is anything but easy.

Still, it wasn't the end of the world. What felt like a huge setback back then was, in hindsight, just a stage.

Somehow, that attitude was already there: money is just colored paper. So why act as if it's everything? The desire to be self employed came from somewhere else — making my own decisions, taking responsibility — not from money.

Sometimes you lose something so you can gain something else later: experience, strength, patience. This attempt failed, yes — but the lessons from it gave me courage to try new things again.

And so this chapter was just a part of my life. Back then it felt huge. Today it's clear: it was smaller than it felt.

That phase was temporary too.

A Single Father

In 1992, after reunification, I met my second wife in Brandenburg. At the time, I was working in field sales as a financial advisor. In the beginning, a lot seemed to fit. We got along well, had plans, dreams, and similar ideas about life. After my first marriage had failed, the desire was strong to do it better this time — more mature, more experienced, with the feeling that I had learned from my mistakes. And for a while, it really did go well.

We built something together. And as a father, I wanted it to be different too: to be more present, to listen more, to live more consciously. That was the plan — and for some time, it worked.

But over the years, the "we" changed. Between work, daily life, and responsibilities, closeness got lost. No big explosion — more like a quiet drifting apart. Almost unnoticed, until one day it was clear: there was no shared path anymore. The marriage lasted eighteen years.

After the separation came the fight over our daughter's custody. Our little one had just turned five when she said at the youth welfare office:

"I want to stay with Daddy."

That sentence burned itself into me. Joy, relief — and at the same time, respect for what was now ahead.

Suddenly I was on my own again. This time with a child who needed me. And with a responsibility that had to be carried — and that could be carried.

For ten years, I was a single father, until I met my wife today. Work, parenting, listening, cooking, comforting, setting boundaries — everything was on my shoulders in that time, and still, I did it with all my heart.

Everyday life was like juggling getting up early, waking my child, making breakfast, taking her to school, going to work, cooking, homework, laundry, cleaning, paperwork — and in the evening, falling into bed exhausted. It was hard, no question. But it was worth it. Every single day.

That time was lived consciously, because it was intense and real. Being a father again — but with a different perspective — for that I was grateful.

Sometimes, when the lights were out and my child was finally asleep, I stayed awake for a long time. Not because I had to. But because I wanted to watch her sleep. Quiet music in the background, thoughts in my head — and already the plan for the next day. In moments like that, there was a clear feeling:

This is good. This is right.

Of course there were days of overwhelm too. Days when everything felt like too much. Days when nothing worked the way it should. But then one look at my child was enough, and the reason was there again. Love is stronger than tiredness.

One sentence stayed with me: "Humans are creatures of habit." At some point, it felt true. The stress became daily life. Daily life became routine. And with routine calm came.

Ten years as a single father. Ten years full of love, work, laughter, learning, worry, and pride — ten years that shaped me.

Today it's clear: it wasn't easy. But it was one of the most valuable times of my life, and the memory of it feels good. And like everything in life, that phase passed too.

When I met my wife today, Silvina, in 2020, it became a lot easier. Until my son moved out in 2025, she helped enormously. For him, she was like a mother — not because she had to be, but because she wanted to. She gave him warmth, stability, and a sense of home. And she gave me calm, support, and the feeling that I no longer had to carry everything alone.

I will never forget that time. Because even if everything in life is temporary, some people and some moments stay in your heart.

Everything is temporary.

Death, Part II

Long after my mother died, my father died as well. He lost his battle with cancer.

This time I was an adult. I had my own family, my own worries, responsibility, my own life — and still, when the news came, it felt as if time stood still for a moment.

The shock was like back then. The grief felt familiar. And yet, something was different. By then, I understood death is part of life. Everyone must go one day, no matter how much we wish it were not true.

In the chapter about my mother, I described how hard it is for a child to grasp death. Back then, I didn't understand that pain changes and doesn't stay the same forever. As an adult, I did. I knew that this pain, too, would shift over time — like everything else in life.

My thoughts went back to my father, to the years when he raised us alone: four children, shift work, hardly any free time, little sleep — and still, he was there. Reliable. Strong.

We didn't talk much about feelings. Not him, and not us kids either. And yet we knew how much he loved us. He was a rock in our lives. The way he lived, the courage it took to leave Spain to give us a better future — it shaped me in many ways, especially in learning to be brave.

When he died, there wasn't only sadness. There was gratitude too. Grateful to have had him. Grateful that he didn't have to suffer the way he had been suffering. His final time was spent in the hospital, with no real chance of leaving it again.

Grateful for his strength, his patience, and that tireless will. He carried a lot — and his time, like every time, was limited.

Today I often think of him when difficult decisions are ahead. I ask myself what he would have done. And somehow, he is there then — not visible, not audible, but present.

This goodbye hurt too. It reminds you that everything we love is only with us for a certain time. That doesn't make the loss easier — but it makes it more understandable.

The missing is still there. And yet the pain grew quieter with time. It made room for memories that became brighter.

Now my siblings and I even laugh when we talk about our father — about his stories, about how, as an employee of the German railway, he won countless boxing matches, about his love of motorcycles, about his garden, just to name a few things.

The pain of losing my father isn't gone. But it has changed. Before, it was heavy and dark. Today it is a different color. It doesn't press the way it used to.

And once again, it shows me:

Everything is temporary.

Coming Out

A few years ago, my child — who had been born and raised as my daughter — came out as transgender.

The sweet girl with long hair who always wore pink suddenly cut their hair short and started wearing only black. The time of braids, "Hey sweetheart," and those little cuddly moments seemed to be over overnight. I was shocked, unsure, and to be honest, I didn't know how to handle it.

And there was something else: my head was chaos. Endless questions. Fear of doing something wrong. And that deep worry that my child might suffer, because the world out there isn't always kind.

But pretty quickly one thing became clear to me: the love stays. No matter what it looks like. No matter what name or role my child chooses. From that moment on, I stood behind my then daughter — my son today.

During that time, I was reminded again that even life phases like this, as life changing as they may be, don't last forever. They too are temporary, like everything in life.

It wasn't an easy time. It took four years until my son received the required medical letter that allowed him to begin testosterone treatment. During those years, he went through highs and lows, and I did my best to stand by his side. Sometimes it was hard — for him, and for me as well.

I had to learn to let go. To understand identity in a new way. And to accept that love has nothing to do with labels.

Today our relationship is closer than ever. We talk openly, laugh a lot, and respect each other.

My son is strong and honest, and I'm incredibly proud of him. He has taught me more about courage than I could have ever found in books.

When I look back now, I see that every difficult phase — as painful as it was — brought us closer in the end. I understood that real love means accepting the other person in their full truth. Not only when it's easy, but especially when it takes courage.

And every time I look at him, I think: how beautiful that you had the courage to become yourself. Because life is too short to be anyone else.

What the future will bring in this regard, I don't know. But I'm here — by his side.

Because everything is temporary.

The Value of This Moment

We often chase things that are far ahead of us — goals, plans, expectations. And while we do that, we overlook what is happening right in front of us: this moment.

Many people live in the future or in the past. They think about what was, or about what might come.

But life only ever happens in this one now — in this short moment that is barely here, and in the next second is already part of the past. That's exactly why it is so valuable.

Sometimes it's a small moment that brings more peace than all the big plans. A sunbeam falling through the window. The quiet hum of the coffee machine in the morning. The laughter of children when I get them laughing in my classes as a martial arts instructor. Nothing spectacular — and yet it's everything that matters.

And I notice how much Silvina has changed my way of seeing. Through her I learned to look more closely again. To admire the moon. To watch clouds as they change color. Not to let sunsets just pass by. Even the garden shows me this: it looks different depending on the season. The plants change. Everything lives. Everything shifts. And suddenly, this moment becomes something I enjoy more consciously.

I believe the value of a moment lies in the fact that it never returns. Even if the sun shines again tomorrow, it will shine differently than it does today. We notice that again and again when my wife and I spend time in the garden in the morning — on purpose, with attention. We'll be older. Maybe happier. Maybe more thoughtful. But never exactly the same.

Many people chase "big happiness" and don't notice that it lives in the small moments. Happiness is rarely loud. Often it hides in quietness — in a breath, in a short pause, in the awareness that this moment is a gift. Sometimes it's as simple as a look into the coffee brown eyes of my wife — and suddenly everything is there, without needing anything else.

When you recognize that, you stop waiting for "someday." You start living now — and life becomes simpler. You need less to feel full.

A single moment of awareness can change more than a whole year of rushing.

Because when you see the moment, you begin to understand life itself.

The value of this moment is that it's temporary.

The Search for the Fan

My wife regularly misplaces things. A lighter. Her phone. Her reading glasses. Her keys. Anything you constantly need in everyday life.

And then it starts. She rushes through the house, opens drawers, checks bags — and sometimes even the fridge. And most of the time I get pulled in too, to help search.

Because I've watched this little show repeat itself countless times over the years — and because everything always turns up in the end — I now just laugh and say:

"Amor, it's only temporarily lost. It'll show up again, like it always does."

A typical scene: after this chapter about temporarily lost things was written, my wife got it as a sample to read. We both laughed at how well the sentence "everything is temporary" works in our everyday life.

That same evening we went to dinner in the hotel restaurant. We were on vacation in Alicante. The food was excellent, the atmosphere calm and pleasant. After that, we wanted to go for a walk.

Right before we left, she said, "Please bring me my fan, Amor. It's still 28 degrees and the air is humid."

The question came automatically: "Where is it?"

Her answer: "On the bed, on the dresser, in my handbag, or in one of the beach bags we used today."

In my head, one sentence lit up:

Oh no. This is going to be fun.

So we went up to the room and started searching. Bed, closets, bags. Everything turned upside down. No fan. After ten minutes I sent a WhatsApp message:

"The fan is temporarily lost."

When we came back downstairs, we both laughed.

And the next morning — hard to believe — the fan was sitting peacefully on the nightstand. As if it had never been gone.

Sometimes life is exactly like that. Things disappear. People get upset. You search like crazy. And in the end, everything shows up again.

And that's the lesson of this little story: even what we think is lost is usually only gone for a while.

I have to admit, I wasn't much better in the past. The only difference is this: when I call out, "Amor, do you know where my... is?" after I've desperately searched for a tool or whatever it is, it usually takes only a moment before she grins and puts it right into my hand.

So far, everything we've lost has only ever been temporarily lost.

At the Beach

We were sitting on the beach in La Vila Joiosa, on Spain's Costa Blanca. The sun was warm on our skin, the sea kept its steady rhythm. A perfect moment to keep writing my book, *Alles ist temporär.*

I had just typed a few lines when my wife asked, "Amor, are you working on your book right now?"

"Yes," I said.

She laughed and said, "Then you should also do what you're writing about. Enjoy the moment. Because it's temporary."

We both laughed. I set the laptop aside, we got up, and we jumped into the sea together.

The water was cool, the moment light, full of joy. And suddenly it was crystal clear — exactly what I'm writing about: life, the moment, the now.

Sometimes you don't need big words. Sometimes it's enough to remember that the here and now is all we truly have. This moment — the laughter, the sun, the water — all of it is unique, and it will never come back in the exact same way.

And that's the heart of this book: writing about life is beautiful. But living life is more important. Because life is like the ocean. It moves. It changes. It never stands still. And every jump into it, every breath, every wave is proof of this:

Everything is temporary.

Does Traffic Get on Your Nerves?

Ever since I was young, riding a motorcycle has been part of my life — but only in good weather. Among bikers, that makes me the "fair weather rider," because I only go out when the sun plays along. Anyone who rides knows the feeling: freedom, speed, wind on your skin — and at the same time, the constant attention you need.

There were times when there was a lot of anger in it too, especially toward car drivers.

"Can't he see me?"

"He's not really pulling out right now!"

More than once, those sentences were shouted loudly into my helmet.

Back then it was hard to understand how careless some people can drive. You try to do everything right: stay visible, ride defensively, be careful — and still you end up in those situations where, as a biker, you almost get overlooked. Then it starts: getting angry, gesturing, swearing — and sometimes the feeling even sticks around for days.

Only later, when I was more often out in a car myself, something important happened:

I started making the same mistakes too.

Not out of malice — simply because in a car, you really do miss things. A motorcycle is smaller, more agile, and often quicker than your eyes expect. And suddenly I was the one my younger self would have gotten mad at.

That was a turning point. Because it became clear: anger changes nothing. It only eats energy — energy you could use for something better.

Over time, more calmness came. And it felt good.

Today I tell my children, who ride motorcycles too: “As a biker, you have to look for two — for yourself and for the other driver. Ride like you’re going to be overlooked.” That sentence has stayed with us.

Of course there are still moments that are annoying: people tailgating, honking, cutting in, or using their phone while driving. But staying calm helps more. Because what would getting angry change? The other person often doesn’t even notice — and in the end, it only hurts one person: you.

In the past, I would have gestured, maybe even provoked. Today, one deep breath is enough, and one thought:

This is just a moment.

And that’s the truth. A short instant. A tiny fraction, compared to all the hours, days, and years life holds. So why waste energy on something that will be over in a second anyway?

Calmness is a form of strength. Staying quiet when others get loud. Smiling where others curse. If you can do that, you’ve understood what really matters.

The anger on the road passes — like everything else. And the more often you remember that, the less anything bothers you at all. Because even in traffic, the rule is the same:

Everything is temporary.

Change

In my view, change is the only thing in life that truly stays constant.

Everything around us shifts — people, places, feelings, thoughts. Even what looks unshakable doesn't remain the way it was. And even though everyone knows that somewhere deep down, it still scares many people. So we hold on: to habits, to relationships, to routines that feel safe. But life isn't a still image. It's moving.

Over the years, I understood something: change isn't something to fear. It's like a wave. If you try to stop it, it will roll right over you. But if you learn to move with it, it carries you.

Sometimes change comes quietly — as a thought, a small decision, a meeting that shifts something inside you. And sometimes it hits with full force — through loss, separation, illness, or the death of someone you love. No matter how it shows up, one thing happens almost every time: it forces you to look. And that is where its power lies.

There were many moments when I thought, why now? The meaning often only showed itself later. And some things that felt like setbacks were, in truth, new beginnings. Something old had to end so something new could begin.

Change isn't always comfortable, but it's necessary. Without change, there is no growth. We would stay stuck — out of comfort, or out of fear. But life wants movement. It wants development.

Maybe the secret is not to fight change, but to understand it. It isn't an enemy. It's a teacher. And like every teacher, it shows you things you don't always want to see. Once that really sinks in, change loses its threat. It becomes what it truly is: a natural part of life.

Today I handle upheavals more calmly. They come anyway — whether you're ready or not. And one thing is just as clear: every phase, every turning point, every movement is temporary.

Nothing stays the same forever — and that's a good thing.

Because life means change. And change means:

Everything is temporary.

Health – The Greatest Gift

Health. What could be more important?

When you look back, you quickly see what gets lost when your body stops cooperating: pain, less mobility, dependence on others, fear — and sometimes financial stress too. That's why this topic deserves its own chapter. Because work, possessions, or recognition suddenly feel small when your health is gone.

1. Why is health so fragile

In everyday life, a lot of strain quietly builds up. Too little movement. Poor sleep. Unhealthy food. Constant stress. On top of that come environment, genetics — and sometimes simply bad luck.

And often you notice it late. Many problems start quietly and grow over years. Until your body says one day:

Enough.

2. What many people struggle with in Germany

When you look at statistics, the same topics come up again — for example back pain, high blood pressure, and metabolic issues like elevated cholesterol.

A quick note: some of the figures and examples people commonly refer to here are based on German data and the German health context, so they may not translate one to one to every country.

The tricky part is this: a lot of it doesn't hurt much at first. Or you get used to it. And that's how it slips through.

Health isn't something you "own" once and then you're done. It's more like a bank account. You can make deposits — or keep withdrawing until one day there's nothing left.

3. Smoking — and why it's not a game

Smoking is one of the biggest risks to health. Cigarette smoke contains many toxic and cancer-causing substances — for example benzene, formaldehyde, carbon monoxide, and ammonia. Lists often mention substances like arsenic or cadmium as well.

These are not "small harmless things." They attack the airways, the heart and circulatory system, and cells — and they increase cancer risk, among other things.

4. What I learned personally

In my martial arts school, I've seen one thing again and again over the years: people who think "it'll be fine" often realize too late that the body suffers quietly for a long time before it gets loud.

For me it went like this: I started smoking at fifteen. In my group back then, it was "cool." I had no idea what I was really doing to myself.

At twenty-two, someone asked me a simple question:

"Why do you smoke?

There was no smart answer.

So, I took the cigarette pack, threw it — with the remaining cigarettes — into the trash, and never smoked again.

And yes: it was a small decision with a big effect. It still reminds me today that even bad habits are temporary — if you're willing to end them.

Because this topic matters to me, I also want to recommend a book that truly helped in our home: "Mein Geschenk für deine genussvolle Raucherentwöhnung" by Peter Kruse.

It's not written in a dry way. It's motivating and easy to understand. My wife, Silvina, used it to quit smoking.

5. What you can do today is no pressure, no perfection. Just take an honest look:

- How is your movement?

- How is your sleep?

- How often has stress become "normal"?

- If you smoke or are used to smoke: what could it take long term?

And most importantly: be grateful for your body. Treat it well. Health is not guaranteed. It's a huge gift.

And like everything in life: temporary.

My Purpose in Life

What is the purpose of life, if we are all only here for such a short time on this beautiful planet? Many people search their whole lives for an answer.

Over time, something became clear to me: purpose isn't somewhere "out there." It's created where you do something good.

For me, that means making a small contribution — helping people become stronger, not only physically, but inside. As a trainer, I see it every day: someone walks out of the school after training a little more upright. Their eyes are clearer. Their shoulders lift because confidence grows. And then I feel it:

This is right. This matters.

Martial arts, for me, is more than technique, discipline, and movement. It's a school of life. It teaches courage, respect, patience, and awareness — with others, and with yourself. You learn to fall and get back up. You learn to stand your ground without becoming arrogant. And you realize that true strength isn't in fighting — it's in understanding.

So, when the question comes — what is the purpose of my life? The answer is simple: helping people discover their confidence, showing them that there is more inside them than they believe.

And if, in the end, someone simply walks through life a little straighter — with a calmer look and more inner peace — then my part is fulfilled.

But purpose isn't only about being there for others. It's also about using the moment — enjoying it, experiencing it. Because at some point it became truly clear: Everything is temporary.

So, there is less time for worries about things that may never happen, and less energy for things you can't change. Not because it doesn't matter — but because it doesn't help. And because it helps neither me nor anyone else.

Time should flow where it has meaning to family, to friends, to people who matter. Time with them is precious.

And there is something else I'm grateful for: I can earn my living with my passion. Enough for a house, a car, vacations, and a good life. Wealth was never the goal — because nobody takes any of it with them. We leave the way we came:

With empty pockets.

So why waste valuable lifetime just to pile up unnecessary money or things? To me, what matters more is what is lived, what is given, and with whom that time is shared.

Maybe that is the purpose. Not trying to change the whole world — but making an impact in small ways. With heart. With humility. With awareness.

Because what we give remains for a moment.

And that moment counts.

Even if it is temporary.

What Remains When Everything Passes

The older I get, the clearer one thing becomes: so much in life is a question of perspective. What irritates you, hurts you, or makes you anxious today often carries hardly any weight a few weeks, months, or years from now. It fades. It moves to the background. And maybe that is exactly where a great relief lives.

Again and again, you notice how differently people react to the same situation. What knocks one person completely off balance, another shrugs off. Often it isn't about what happened, but about how it is seen. Everyone carries their own world inside.

Many people believe happiness is somewhere "out there" — in things, in success, in recognition. But it rarely feels that way in real life. Happiness is more likely to appear in moments of clarity. In those short seconds when you stop searching for a moment. It isn't a permanent state. It's brief, honest, quiet — and in those seconds, you simply are.

And life doesn't wait until we're ready. It happens, just like that. And whoever tries to control everything will eventually grow tired. Of course we want safety, stability, predictability. But life is movement — and movement means change.

Sometimes it feels as if everything has to be understood. But not everything needs an explanation. Some things are meant to be lived: being sad, doubting, being quiet. That belongs just as much as joy or success.

Maybe wisdom is nothing more than making peace with what cannot be changed. And over time, you also see: even heavy phases have their place. They make us softer, calmer — sometimes even more grateful.

My need to have everything under control has become smaller. Instead, it's more about living consciously. Feeling the moment without immediately forcing meaning onto it. Because every thought, every feeling, every person we meet is only part of our path for a certain time.

That is what makes it so beautiful. And sometimes so painful. But that is life.

And life means letting go, getting back up, and continuing.

Because in the end, all that remains is the memory that everything is temporary.

Farewell

"Dear friends and family,

today we have come together to say goodbye to our friend…

Here among us are his family, his wife, and his daughter… as well as former colleagues from the medical field, friends, and the members of his Wing Chun group.

I am speaking now on behalf of that Wing Chun group.

In 2001, dear …, you began training Wing Chun with us. Around twenty five years have passed since then. Years in which you did not only love this martial art — you lived it.

In the Philippines, you even set up your own training room, with a wooden dummy, training equipment, and all of your certificates.

You once asked me to build you a Wing Chun dummy. You wanted to place it in your second apartment in Berlin.

I agreed to build it. But there was always "something in the way" — a renovation here, exam preparation there — and I kept thinking: I still have time.

In the end, I didn't have time.

I set the wrong priorities and I didn't fulfill your wish. I missed that opportunity, and that is exactly where you see that everything in life is temporary.

I regret it deeply.

You accompanied me, and all of us, to seminars across Europe — in France, Portugal, England, and many other places.

Your enthusiasm was always high, and throughout all those years you never stopped training.

You even managed to inspire your daughter … to practice Wing Chun. She didn't just take on your passion — she showed exceptional talent.

Training with her was always something special for me. It would be a great honor to continue her education and to deepen her Wing Chun on the path you began with her.

Only your beloved wife … you could never convince — even though we often spoke about it together with a smile.

… was not only my student and training partner, he was also my dentist.

I remember a root canal treatment in his practice. When he noticed that something hurt, he asked, 'Does it hurt, Mario?' — and I answered with a smile: 'Yes, it hurts. But don't worry, you'll get it back at the next training session.'

That memory also shows the humorous side of our friendship — a side that did all of us good.

As human beings, we often think we have all the time in the world. But we don't. Everything is temporary.

During our twenty five years together, I never truly thought about the fact that one day it could end.

As recently as July 2025, we met in the city park in Duisburg Rheinhausen to train together — full of hope that we would see each other more regularly again in the future.

Now things have turned out differently.

What remains are our memories, and the lesson: everything is temporary. We never know when it will be the 'last time.'

So let us — those of us who are allowed to stay a little longer on this small planet — be grateful.

Grateful for the time we have been given. Let us try to live it as fully and as happily as we can.

… and I present you, in recognition of your work as an instructor and as part of our Wing Chun Pai — our Wing Chun family — with the certificate and belt for Black Belt of the Close Range Combat Academy.

…, your Wing Chun path continues in us — in every training session, in every technique, in every memory.

Your passion lives on in us, and it will never end.

We love you."

That was my funeral speech…

The words "everything is temporary" often make me sad. Goodbyes are part of life, even though we would rather avoid them. Sometimes they come quietly. Sometimes with full force. But they always come. Whether it's the loss of a person, a friend leaving, the end of a love, or simply leaving a familiar place — every goodbye leaves traces.

I have experienced many goodbyes in my life. Some were final. Others were only temporary. But no matter how they arrived, they changed me every time. In the beginning there is almost always pain — that feeling of emptiness and loss — and you believe that this emptiness will never go away.

But it does. Slowly, step by step.

I learned that letting go doesn't mean forgetting. It means accepting that something is over — and in that acceptance, there is peace.

Often we fear goodbyes because we believe what comes afterward must be worse. But life taught me otherwise. Every ending carries a beginning inside it. You just don't see it right away, because your eyes are still fixed on what has been.

I remember many moments when I thought, that's it. Everything is different now. And yes, it was different. But different is not always bad. Different is simply new. And the new is what helps us grow.

Sometimes we have to let people go — not because we don't love them anymore, but because their time in our life is over. Understanding that wasn't easy. But once you truly understand it, goodbye loses part of its fear.

Today I see farewell differently. I know that everything that was truly important keeps a place inside me — in memories, in thoughts, in what I learned from it. I also know that one day I will be part of a goodbye myself — and that's okay.

Because farewell doesn't simply mean "end." It means change. It's a transition. A quiet reminder that everything we love is only on loan.

And when you accept that, the pain grows quieter and gratitude grows louder.

Because even the deepest farewell is not forever — it only changes its tone, like everything in life.

Everything is temporary.

The Wall

While I was writing this book, I often thought about what the cover should look like. Nothing felt right. No idea stuck. So I asked my youngest son, who had just started studying art, to help me.

Because "everything is temporary," he suggested using a wall as the foundation — a wall that slowly crumbles and falls apart. I was instantly excited, because that image fit the heart of my book perfectly.

When I saw the first drafts, I couldn't help thinking of the Berlin Wall. And that's how the idea for this chapter was born.

When the Berlin Wall fell in 1989, it felt far away to me back then — almost like something that happened in another country. And yet it was only about 300 kilometers to what we now call the eastern federal states. But as a teenager, I wasn't interested in politics. It was what it was, and I thought you couldn't change anything anyway.

I could never have imagined that years later people would lovingly call me a "Wossi" — a mix of "Wessi" and "Ossi."("Wessi" is a nickname for people from the west of Germany, while "Ossi" is a nickname for people from the east of Germany). Later on, I spent a lot of time in the East, sometimes even more than in the West. Some of my friends had relatives there and visited them now and then. And to us it felt like it would stay that way forever.

But then came 1989.

On the news you saw people in Leipzig, Dresden, and Berlin taking to the streets. They shouted, "We are the people," and demanded freedom. Back then I didn't fully understand what was happening, but I could feel that something was shifting. And then, on November 9th, the Wall came down.

Like so many others, I sat in front of the television and could hardly believe it. People danced, cried, hugged each other. A whole nation was suddenly free.

In 1991, I traveled to East Germany for the first time myself. It was a shock — and at the same time a wonderful experience. The streets, houses, and shops looked old. A lot was broken. But the people were warm, friendly, and helpful. You could feel a kind of togetherness that I didn't know like that. Everyone helped everyone.

Rents were around 20 to 60 Deutsche Mark, wages around 300 to 500 Deutsche Mark. To me, that was unimaginable. It felt like another world.

I remember long lines outside the Konsum, the local store. People stood outside early in the morning when you heard, "Tomorrow we'll have bananas." And still, they carried a kind of contentment and warmth that deeply impressed me.

Over the years, friendships grew — in Mecklenburg Western Pomerania, in Brandenburg where I met my second wife, and in Thuringia, where my best friend lives with his family.

When I drive to Bad Salzungen today, I often think, wow. Everything is neat, modern, and beautiful. Streets, shops, houses — everything looks new and clean. When I drive through NRW, sadly, I can't always say the same. The East has caught up — maybe in many areas it has even overtaken.

My second wife, who was born in Brandenburg, grew up right in the middle of that old system. Through her, I gained an insight into life in the GDR. She told me, "Everyone had a job. We were in the FDJ — the Free German Youth. We helped each other." It sounded like community, like solidarity. But under the surface, there was also fear and control.

People spoke in whispers about the Stasi, the state security service — an organization that watched everything and everyone. "If you spoke badly about the system, or said you weren't allowed to travel, you had to expect trouble," she explained.

Many people simply said, "It is what it is. We can't change it." But it could be changed.

Between 1961 and 1989, everything looked fixed — and still, it was only temporary. Everything was temporary.

Even cars were a special topic. If you wanted to buy a Trabant, lovingly called a "Trabi," you sometimes had to wait up to eighteen years. Spare parts were rare. People had to become inventive. They repaired, improvised, found solutions. They learned how to help themselves. That creativity — and that will to make the best out of very little — was impressive.

When I think about all of this today, I see a time full of contrasts: shortage and togetherness, control and courage, loss and new beginnings. The fall of the Wall showed that even systems that seem like they will last forever can end.

Walls fall. Borders disappear. Everything changes.

Freedom doesn't only mean having no walls around you. It also means having no walls in your thinking. All of us sometimes carry borders inside us — old beliefs, fears, habits. But when we are willing to let them go, we realize that change is always possible.

Nothing lasts forever. Everything shifts.

Everything is temporary.

Nail and Axe

Early 1970s. My little brother and I were maybe six and seven years old. Our favorite thing was playing barefoot in the courtyard. And if you read the title of this chapter, you already know: that wasn't always a good idea.

Next to our house, an apartment building was being built. To us, it wasn't a construction site — it was an adventure playground. When the workers weren't there on weekends, we went over to the neighboring lot. There were stones, boards, wooden slats, nails, tar stains — and above all: mud. Lots of it.

We made our own "concrete" from clay and water. We simply called it mud. We glued stones together, built little towers, even tiny walls. They never lasted long, but it was incredibly fun to create something with our own hands. And without anyone calling it that, it also trained creativity.

Walking barefoot on a construction site can end badly sometimes.

At first I didn't even notice anything. Then my brother suddenly looked at me strangely and said, "Mario, you're dragging a piece of wood around."

I looked down. Hanging from my foot was a board about half a meter long. Today I know it was probably a roof batten. Why it was stuck to me was completely unclear. The thought that a long roofing nail had gone through the wood and deep into my heel never even crossed my mind. So I walked — and dragged that board behind me.

First we laughed. It really looked ridiculous, like I was wearing a shoe that was way too big. Maybe I even thought the board was just stuck because of the mud, or because of the black tar that was everywhere.

To free myself, I put my good foot on the batten and tried to lift the other one. It didn't work. My brother said, "Lift your foot, I'll take a look."

So I lifted it. He looked calmly and then said — as if it was the most normal thing in the world:

"You have a nail in your foot."

That was the moment we saw the nail. And only then did the screaming start.

The funny part is: until then, there was no pain. The pain came later, when I limped back to our apartment.

My father was a strong, healthy man. Things were solved the way people had learned to solve them. No doctor. No ambulance. No drama. He looked at my foot and simply said:

"Lie down on the kitchen table. On your back. Foot up."

That's how it was back then.

He disappeared for a moment, then came back with two bottles. One had vinegar. The other was an empty glass bottle. I had no idea what that had to do with my foot — but I was about to find out.

He positioned my foot so the sole was visible and poured vinegar onto the wound. That's when the pain finally caught up with everything it had missed earlier. It burned like fire.

Then came the empty glass bottle. With his left hand he held my ankle tight. With his right hand he hit my heel several times with the edge of the bottle's base.

My only thought was: this is the punishment for being stupid.

I cried my eyes out. He just said, "Don't cry. The hits are only to get the dirt out of the wound. You stepped on a rusty nail."

It didn't take the pain away, but it calmed me. If Dad says it has to be like this, then it probably has to be like this.

In the end, he put a bandage on it — or something like that. And then I went back outside to play.

No doctor. No hospital. No vaccination record in hand. Back then we children hardly saw doctors at all — maybe for a few shots. That was normal.

And now comes the story with the axe.

Don't worry — it won't be that bad. At least not for me. This time it was my little brother again.

At six years old, he loved smashing and breaking things. My father often worked with tools: hammer, axe, crowbar, saw. For my brother, that was heaven.

Often he was even allowed to choose what he wanted to "work" with. Then he sat barefoot on his little greasy butt and happily hit something. Today you might call it "letting off steam." Back then it was simple: kid, tool, and something to hit kept the courtyard quiet.

In the yard, my parents had a shed with rabbits, ducks, and chickens. Above it was a kind of open attic. One day my brother climbed up there with the axe. The plan: to chop up small stones.

He sat down, took the axe in his hands, lifted it over his head, and tried to hit the stone with the sharp side. Of course he missed. Again and again. Not even close.

At some point he changed strategy. What went on in his head, I don't know. Probably something like: I can't hit it with the thin side. Then I'll use the wide side. Problem solving, even back then.

Only one detail was forgotten: when you hold the axe the other way around, the sharp side is now over your own head when you swing.

And he kept swinging.

Down in the courtyard, we couldn't see anything. But we could hear his laughter — happy child laughter. In his world, the new strategy was working.

The pebble was, of course, too hard. A six year old doesn't break stones with an axe. But he had a task, and that was enough.

Then the next thought probably came: I'm hitting it, but not hard enough. So more force. Faster movement. Tired arms. Heavy tool. And then it happened.

The axe slipped. Or he hit himself in the head. We will never know the exact truth.

Down in the yard, everything suddenly went quiet. No chopping. No laughing. Silence. That felt strange to me — and fittingly, we were Spaniards. So I called for him. No answer.

Not truly worried yet, more curious, I climbed up the wooden stairs as a five year old. There he sat. Blood on his hands, his face, his forehead. And what was he doing?

He was playing with it. Smearing it around like it was just another kind of mud.

I was shocked. He wasn't. Maybe it was shock. Maybe it was childhood innocence. When I spoke to him, he smiled at me.

Today that would honestly worry me — a child, covered in blood, smiling. For him it was simply slippery.

The blood slowly ran from a wound on his forehead. Not gushing — but steady.

And what did I shout, completely naturally?

"Dad, we need vinegar and the empty bottle!"

My brother had watched the "nail in the foot" treatment live. When he heard that, he immediately started screaming. In his head, a little horror movie was playing: vinegar in the wound, and then Dad with the glass bottle on his head to "get the dirt out."

Poor kid. The rest was routine: cleaning, vinegar is good, bandage on — and back outside to play.

By now you might be wondering what these crazy childhood stories have to do with the topic of this book.

A lot.

Back then, stepping on a rusty nail or getting a head wound didn't automatically mean going to the doctor. No ambulance. No phone. Not even a landline with a cord — let alone a mobile phone.

The "treatment" was vinegar, a glass bottle, a bandage, and the sentence:

"Go back outside and play."

Today, most parents would probably call an ambulance, or at least drive straight to the emergency room. Tetanus, infection, scar, X ray — maybe even child protection in the back of their mind.

Both are ways of seeing things. Both belong to their time. And that is the point.

Even the way we deal with illness, accidents, and children is temporary. It keeps changing. Thankfully.

What was normal yesterday can look brutal or irresponsible today. And what today is considered the only "right" way might look just as old fashioned in a few decades.

The same is true for parenting styles, fears, trust in technology and systems, and the way we deal with pain. Everything is moving.

When I think of the nail in my heel and the axe story today, I smile. Not because it was harmless — but because it shows how much times change.

Back then, vinegar was the miracle cure. Today, every scratch gets googled. Back then, my father was the ER. Today, there would probably be specialists, machines, and forms involved. Both tell a story about the time we live in.

And that's why this thought fits here too:

Everything is temporary. The methods. The tools. The fears. The safety.

And we are too.

What remains are the stories we make out of it.

And sometimes a few small scars — and years later you smile and say, **"Remember when…?"**

Traffic Jam on the A44

A traffic jam on the A44, Kassel heading toward Dortmund. In front of me and behind me: cars, trucks, headlights. Everything is standing still. Nothing moves.

The engine is off. The lights are off. People get out, walk around on the highway, make calls, nervously tap on their phones.

After a while, the radio announcement comes on:

"The A44 between Erwitte and Soest is closed due to an accident."

About ten minutes later, ambulances, firefighters, tow trucks, and the ADAC roll past us through the median. Sirens wail, blue lights flash. The air is quiet — but tense.

This is one of those moments where many people think: Great. I really didn't need this today.

And yes, I know that thought too. In the past, that's exactly what would have happened: getting restless, drumming on the steering wheel, checking the time, getting annoyed.

Today I stay calm. As these lines are written, I'm sitting right in the middle of the A44 — and I'm relaxed. Why? Because one thing is clear:

Everything is temporary. Even this traffic jam.

Getting upset won't change anything. There's nothing I can do about the situation. No honking, no swearing, no frustration will make the cars in front of me disappear. But there is one thing that always remains: The decision of how you deal with it.

So I use the time.

This chapter is being written right here, in the middle of the highway. And while everything outside is standing still, the thoughts keep moving. Calmness. Patience. The difference between movement and stillness.

Around me, many people look stressed. Some walk back and forth. Others are on the phone. Some just shake their heads.

What for?

We're all stuck in the same jam. We'll all arrive later. And nobody can change that right now.

Maybe life is sometimes exactly like this. You're stuck, even though you want to move forward. It feels like time is being wasted.

But maybe it's just a pause. A chance to breathe for a second.

And if we're honest: being stuck in a traffic jam is not the worst thing that can happen. One look at the situation of those involved in the accident is enough. Then you realize quickly: standing still is sometimes even luck.

Maybe a traffic jam is even a small gift. Unplanned, but there. An opportunity to slow down, to think, to feel — to simply be.

Next time you're stuck, dear reader, try it differently. Take a breath. Lean back. Put on music, or enjoy the quiet. Make the best of the time you have anyway.

And be grateful that you're not the reason for this jam.

[illegible]

A Grain of Sand in the Milky Way

Sometimes it helps to make yourself a little smaller.

Not in the sense of "I'm worthless." But in the sense of: I'm not the center of the universe.

And that's a good thing.

The idea for this chapter didn't come in a fancy office. It came in a simple place — on our construction site. I was standing at the concrete mixer, mixing gravel, cement, and water with my brother and our friend Matthes to build our garage.

In front of me was a big pile of concrete gravel, size 0 to 32 mm. Thousands of little stones. All different — and yet somehow all the same.

And in that moment, one thought came:

If each of these stones were a star or a planet, how small would Earth be? And how small would we humans be on it?

So let's do a thought experiment.

In the Milky Way, there are — by today's estimates — roughly 100 billion stars and at least as many planets. To keep it simple, let's say around 200 billion celestial bodies.

Now we say: one pebble represents one star or one planet.

That means we would need 200 billion pebbles.

That would be around 800 million kilograms — about 800,000 tons of concrete gravel. And transporting it would take roughly 32,000 fully loaded trucks.

Just for our Milky Way.

Not for the whole universe.

Just for one single galaxy among billions of others.

And in that picture, Earth wouldn't even be its own pebble. It would be more like a speck of dust on the surface of a pebble.

Now we look at ourselves.

A person is maybe 1.70 meters tall. Up close, you can see arms, legs, a head. But from about five to six kilometers away, a person is barely visible to the naked eye — and that's only if it's flat land, with no hills, houses, or trees in between. Perfect clear view.

At five or six kilometers, we disappear for the human eye. The Milky Way is about 100,000 light years wide. In kilometers, that's around 946,000,000,000,000,000.

If you let that number sit for a second, you realize quickly: this is a scale our minds can barely hold.

And that's why something else becomes clear:

We are tiny in this enormous whole.

Not just you. Me too. All of us.

And now the question: is it good or bad to be so small, so "unimportant" compared to the universe?

For me, the answer is clear:

It's good.

For one simple reason: it takes a massive weight off your shoulders.

Because people often live as if the world will collapse if something goes wrong. But each of us is a tiny dot on a small planet, on a side branch of a galaxy that itself is only one of billions of galaxies.

That doesn't mean your life has no value.

It only means: not everything has to be controlled. Perfection isn't necessary. Mistakes are allowed.

A few examples:

Embarrassing moments. A stupid sentence. A slip of the tongue. A mistake in front of others. In your head it feels like the end of the world. In reality, many people barely notice. And tomorrow most won't care anymore. Everything is temporary.

Conflict and drama. A fight with someone — in traffic, in the family, at work. In the moment it feels huge. On the scale of the Milky Way, that argument isn't even a grain of sand. Letting go is allowed. Not every battle has to be fought.

Perfectionism. Many people carry the sentence inside: "I'm not allowed to make mistakes." When you realize how small you are in the universe, you also realize: your résumé isn't a cosmic document. No star cares about grades or school history. That can set you free — to try things, to fail, and to see failure as a normal part of life.

Failure and new beginnings. A business goes under. A relationship breaks. A dream collapses. It feels enormous. On the scale of the Milky Way, it's a quick blink. That can comfort you: starting over is possible. Nobody is "failed forever." Because that, too, is temporary.

Fear of what others think. How often do people hold back just because they're afraid of being judged. When you realize we are, together, only a few dust specks on a giant pile of pebbles, the opinions of others lose some of their power. Your life is allowed to be lived.

One difference matters here:

Cosmically, we are tiny. Humanly, we can be infinitely important to each other.

For a child, a loving look from a parent matters more than the size of the Milky Way. For a lonely person, a single hug can mean more than all the stars in the sky.

The universe doesn't ask how your day was.

But you can make another person's day better.

And that's where our chance lies: cosmically we are small — but in our small corner of the world, we can make a big difference.

When you accept that you're not the center of the universe, life gets lighter. Less pressure. Less fear. More freedom to do what truly matters.

And suddenly the sentence fits again:

Everything is temporary.

Worries. Mistakes. Anger.

But also opportunities. Time. The body.

Even the concrete of the garage I mixed will one day crack, weather, and fade away. Nothing stays the way it is. Not the gravel in the mixer. Not you. Not me.

Not even our Milky Way.

And that's why this sentence belongs here too:

Everything is temporary.

Is Everything Really Temporary?

While I was writing this book, I received a message:

"Everything is temporary... as long as you want it to be. It always depends on your own view and attitude. You have no control over feelings!"

I had to read that sentence more than once. Not because it was unclear, but because it triggered something. Maybe there's more truth in it than I wanted to see at first.

The message was clear: not everything disappears just because you believe it will. Some things remain, no matter what you think. Feelings, for example. Memories. Longing. And sometimes you really don't have control over that.

And yes — that's partly true.

When you lose someone, you can't just switch grief off. When love is there, you can't simply turn it off. Some things stay inside us, even when the situation is long over. And maybe that's a good thing.

Still, life shows us something else:

Feelings rarely stay exactly the way they were.

They don't always vanish — but they change shape. Pain becomes insight. Grief becomes memory. Anger becomes calm. And love becomes gratitude.

So maybe it's not about things disappearing. Maybe it's about transformation.

Nothing stays the way it was. Not even what sits deep inside us.

Some things take years. Others take seconds. But everything is moving. Everything changes.

And now comes the part that matters to me here: I don't want to tell you what to believe. I just want to invite you to pause for a moment and ask yourself:

What does "temporary" mean to you?

What in your life has come — and gone again?

What changed, even though you thought it would last forever?

And what about your feelings: do they really stay the same, or have they slowly transformed over time?

Maybe you lost someone, and you still feel the grief today. Maybe there's a memory that instantly stirs something in you. Maybe you carry something that hasn't gone away — but has become quieter.

And maybe you're holding on to something because you believe you have to. Or maybe you've learned to let go because you realized it helps you.

Which one is true for you?

Because that's what this is really about: not a perfect answer, but an honest look inward.

I can understand when someone says, "Everything is temporary, as long as you want it to be." Because yes — your attitude matters. It matters whether you are ready to let go or whether you keep holding on.

Maybe in the end it's both: will and change.

You can decide how long you hold on to something. But you can't stop it from changing.

And maybe that's the core of it: even if we don't let go, life will eventually do it for us. It shifts, transforms, renews — quietly, but steadily.

Maybe both sides are right: the thought that some things remain, and the insight that everything changes.

In the end, it's not about who is right.

It's about giving your own thoughts space.

And if you become quiet for a moment after this chapter and ask yourself what in your life was temporary — or still is — then this chapter has done its job.

Time Is Relative

Albert Einstein once said, "Time is relative." A sentence meant scientifically — but it's also true in everyday life.

Time doesn't feel the same for everyone. An hour at the dentist can feel like an eternity. The same hour with someone you love is suddenly over, as if it were only five minutes. Sometimes time stretches. Sometimes it slips through your fingers.

When you're waiting, it drags. When you're living something beautiful, it runs. And one day you stand there and ask yourself: where did all those years go?

You see it constantly in daily life. Eight hours in a job you don't enjoy can feel endless. Eight hours spent with passion, joy, and purpose can pass in the blink of an eye.

This understanding helps me sometimes to be more patient. Because when you realize time is relative, a lot loses its pressure. You rush less. You get less irritated. You become calmer.

There were phases when days felt heavy — worry, grief, overwhelm. And in the middle of it you think: this will never end.

And yet it passed.

Just like everything passes.

Even hard hours are only sections of the road.

And then there are the other times — the ones you want to hold on to because they are light, warm, alive.

But they pass too. And that's exactly what makes them so valuable.

Time is relative. It flows. It changes. And again and again it shows us: nothing stays the way it is.

Maybe that's where the meaning is.

You can't hold time — but you can use it, as long as it is yours.

Because time itself is temporary.

The Phone

Sometimes I wonder when we stopped truly listening. When we started looking at a screen instead of into the eyes of the person sitting right in front of us.

I see it everywhere. In training, in cafés, in families, in groups of friends. Parents staring at their phones while their kids are doing sports. Teenagers sitting next to each other but barely saying a word. Couples going out to eat and both silently scrolling through their feeds.

It's as if we forgot how to really be present.

Sometimes I joke and say, "You're sitting across from each other. You can talk. You don't have to text." And everyone laughs.

The phone is long past being "just a device." It's an alarm clock, a calendar, a camera, a message center — and an escape route all at once. A constant companion. Always within reach. Always important.

And that's exactly where the problem starts.

While we're constantly online, we often miss the life that's happening right in front of us.

One scene from training stayed with me. A child proudly showed a technique they had just learned. The child looked at the mother, searching for her eyes. But she was typing a message. When she looked up for a second, the moment was already gone. The child turned around and continued.

No drama. No words. Just that small sting — the kind you can't see, but you can feel. And it doesn't only affect parents. All of us are part of it now. How often does someone sit in front of us, telling us something, and we only half nod? Half there. Half somewhere else. How often do we scroll without thinking, instead of looking into the real face right in front of us?

From my point of view, the phone itself isn't the real problem.

It's what's underneath it.

I think many of us can barely tolerate silence anymore. Because silence isn't empty. In silence, you hear yourself. And it's not always peaceful. There are thoughts, pressure, worries, unfinished topics — sometimes even loneliness. The phone makes it easy to run away from that. One grab, one swipe, and you don't have to feel.

The second reason is habit. We got used to filling every tiny gap immediately. Waiting at the checkout. Sitting in the car. A five minute break. That used to be time.

Today it's "wasted time" — time that has to be stuffed with content.

The third reason is this constant feeling of "I have to be reachable." Everything could be important. Everything could be urgent. And that's exactly how it feels. The phone turns every moment into a little state of alert. Even when nothing is happening, the mind stays on standby:

Something could come in.

And then there's another reason many people don't like to admit:

We crave validation.

A like. A message. A sign that we're seen. That's human. But when you become dependent on it, you start missing real closeness. You sit next to each other — and you're not really there.

In the end, the phone is often a shield. It protects us from boredom, restlessness, feelings, conversations, decisions. It makes life easier — but also flatter.

And suddenly you notice: I'm constantly busy, but I'm not truly connected. Not to others. And sometimes not even to myself.

And yes, I catch myself too. Too often my fingers automatically reach for the phone. For no reason. Out of habit. Out of boredom. Or simply because distraction has become so easy.

But something important happens in silence.

Real listening. Real seeing. That feeling of: I'm truly here.

Sometimes I put the phone down on purpose. And then I notice how quiet everything becomes — and how much you suddenly take in when nothing keeps interrupting. A smile. A look. A conversation that deepens.

All of it is there.

We just overlook it too often.

Maybe we should remind ourselves more often: no post, no like, no message is more important than the person sitting with us right now. Because one day, this moment is gone. And what you didn't truly live, doesn't come back.

The phone can wait.

Life can't.

Even attention is temporary. And if we give it away, it should be a conscious choice.

What Remains?

In the end, what remains isn't what we owned — it's what we shared, what we taught, and what we loved.

We don't leave behind things.

We leave traces.

A smile. A piece of advice. A memory. Maybe a gesture that gave someone strength. Or a sentence that showed up at exactly the right moment.

So many people spend their whole lives chasing the same thing: more money, more security, more value. They work, save, invest. Houses, cars, accounts — always with the feeling: if I have that, then I'm safe.

But in the end, one thing becomes clear: on that day — the day everything ends — nobody takes any of it with them. Everything we "own" is only with us for a while. Money, possessions, status, success — it's temporarily "ours." Borrowed.

And sooner or later, it gets handed back.

We forget that easily. Then we cling, as if things could hold us steady. But even those things are only companions for a time.

The real value isn't in having.

It's in being — and in giving.

Maybe what we call "possessions" isn't what matters at all. Maybe true wealth is how many people were touched. How much love was given. How often someone felt hope because of you.

Those are the things that live on when we're already gone.

Things fade. Memories remain. Possessions can be inherited — but not the warmth of a smile.

Once you truly understand that, life gets lighter. Then it's no longer about how much you have.

It's about how much you gave.

What remains is what we shared.

Everything else was only temporary.

Looking Back

When I look back today, I'm amazed at how quickly everything passed.

As a father of three children, I lived through very different seasons. There were phases when two of my kids were mostly with me only on weekends. And later there were years when I raised one child alone while the other two were already grown.

Each chapter was different.

And each one mattered in its own way.

There were those weekends you wait for all week — laughter, outings, small adventures, movie nights, conversations… sometimes serious, sometimes silly. And when Sunday evening comes, you ask every time:

Where did the time go?

Later, when I was again the father of a small child, I understood even more clearly how precious these moments are. A child sleeping. Laughing. Asking questions. Simply being there.

Those are moments you will never get back in exactly the same way. They pass quietly, almost unnoticed. And one day, there stands a young person with their own path.

Over time I learned not to count the days, but to feel them. Not to wait for children to finally get older, but to live the moment while they are still small. Because what feels normal today is already a memory tomorrow.

Parents plan a lot — work, appointments, responsibilities.

Children live in the now.

For them, it doesn't matter how much you got done. What matters is whether you were there.

And for me, that's the greatest gift you can give your children:

Time.

I'm grateful for every hour I was allowed to be a father. For every smile. Every "Dad." For that normal life that keeps bringing you back to what truly matters.

Because one thing is certain: time with your children passes faster than you think.

And it doesn't come back.

So enjoy every moment.

Because this time, too, is temporary.

When Children Leave

At some point the day comes when the child you raised moves out — the moment you avoid thinking about for a long time, because deep down you know: it's coming.

And still, when it happens, it feels as if a piece of your life is suddenly packing a suitcase.

When my last child moved out at nineteen, they looked at me and asked, "So what are you going to do now without me?"

My answer came right away: "Cry all day."

We both laughed — and at the same time it was clear: there was more truth in that joke than you want to admit.

In the weeks before, I heard the question more than once: "How are you dealing with it? With the move. With the new city."

And honestly? Not well.

It felt strange after so many years. The house became quieter. The daily rhythm slower. Almost too quiet. Something was missing — something that had become so normal: small everyday sounds, a voice from a bedroom, a quick sentence in the kitchen.

In that time, I was grateful not to be alone. My wife, Silvina, was there. She carried me through those days. She caught me when it felt heavy. And she kept reminding me that life goes on. Just not having to carry it all inside myself made a big difference.

And then, step by step, another thought came:

This is part of life too.

You don't raise children to hold on to them. You raise them so they can go. That's the point — even if it hurts.

Letting go doesn't mean it didn't matter.

Letting go means trusting — in what you gave them, and in life itself.

When I look back, there were many moments in life where I had to let go: relationships, places, people, jobs, situations. Often it hurt. And every time, sooner or later, space appeared for something new.

It's the same here.

The heart needs time to adjust.

But it grows with every change.

That evening, alone in the living room, the thought returned that has followed me since the beginning of this book:

Everything is temporary.

But maybe that is exactly where the beauty is. When nothing lasts, you learn to love the moment instead of trying to hold it.

When children leave, love remains.

And even this pain is temporary.

A Quiet New Beginning

When my son moved out, a new chapter began — not just for him, but for us at home too. For him it was a fresh start: his own life, a new environment, a new city, his own household, new faces, university beginning. A mix of curiosity, excitement, freedom, and uncertainty.

I felt proud. And at the same time there was that quiet moment:

So it's really happening.

Before our nineteen year old moved, my wife and I drove to Dortmund regularly to help him. Renovating the apartment, assembling furniture, setting up the kitchen, painting walls, fixing small things. Those trips kept us busy. They gave the transition structure. You were still in it, you still had a task, and you could feel it:

We're walking with him into this.

And then suddenly it was like this: he lives there now, and we live here.

All at once there was more space. More order. More quiet. And at first, that felt unfamiliar.

It wasn't just the big things. It was the small ones.

The shoes in the hallway suddenly stood there as a pair. At night the lights stayed off more often. Nobody called out from a room, "Can you just…?" Nobody walked into the kitchen just to grab something and throw out a quick joke.

When we went shopping, the bags filled more slowly. The receipts got shorter. And at the same time our eyes began to notice different things. We bought differently, thought differently, planned differently.

These changes happen quietly. You don't even notice them — until one day you do:

This is our new everyday life.

In the beginning, the quiet sometimes felt nice. And sometimes it carried something that felt like longing. Not painful. Just new. A silence that leaves room — for thoughts, for memories, for that quick look back:

Remember how it used to be?

With time it became clear: this is a new beginning too. Not only for the child, but for us as well. Time that used to be naturally filled by family slowly starts filling in a different way now. Walks. Conversations. Shared calm. More "us."

And still, family doesn't disappear. It only changes its shape.

Daily togetherness becomes a different kind of togetherness. "Can you come here for a second?" becomes "Give me a quick call." Everyday life becomes a visit you look forward to. Closeness becomes trust.

Sometimes I look at the space where there used to be more life and think: how fast that all happened. And then pride comes back — because what we gave holds.

Our child is walking his path.

And we keep walking ours.

Maybe that's the next step: not less family, but a new form of family. Now it's about looking forward. Not holding on, but accepting. Staying open to what comes — to new things, to change, to life itself.

I want to experience what life gives as consciously as I can. Not rushing. Not sprinting. Seeing, feeling, hearing, living — so that one day I can look back and smile and think:

Yes. That was good.

Even if it was only temporary.

The Road to My First Book

My first book, *The Art of Wing Chun*, (Die Kunst des Wing Chun) didn't just happen.

It was a long road. Ten years of work. Doubts. Breaks. Restarts. Small wins and big questions. Ten years where the thought often came up:

Where is this even going?

There were times full of energy — endless ideas, real excitement. I would sit at my desk and the thoughts would flow. Page after page became something that felt right.

And then came the other days. An empty head. Everyday life breathing down your neck. Or simply no desire at all. Then the questions showed up: Who is this book for? Which topics belong in it? How should the chapters be built? Which drawings, photos, and examples truly fit?

Sometimes I wrote the first lines, read them the next day, and deleted everything. Then the project sat still for weeks until a new thought, an experience, or a conversation brought me back to the desk.

During that time I understood something:

Inspiration doesn't always come on its own.

Sometimes you have to stay seated even when the words don't come. Sometimes discipline matters more than motivation. And sometimes one small spark is enough to make the fire burn again.

Quitting was never my thing. Not for decades. Endurance is part of the art — not only in Wing Chun, but in writing too. Both need patience, clarity, and dedication.

Today I hold *The Art of Wing Chun* in my hands. And when I look back on those ten years, I know: every hour, every doubt, every pause had meaning.

It was a process, not a sprint. A journey that shaped me — as a teacher, as a person, and as an author.

And like everything in life, that time was not endless. The long hours at the desk, the sleepless nights, the back and forth in my mind — all of it was only a season.

Maybe that's the best part of it: something that took so much time is now here — in words, in thoughts, in the hands of those who read it.

Because even the effort fades.

But what we create can remain.

It was hard. It was a lesson. It was temporary.

Blessed to Do What I Love

Sometimes you look at your life and wonder how it all happened. And then the beginnings come back: small training rooms, simple conditions, days when only a handful of students showed up for class.

Back then, Wing Chun was mostly passion. More heart than plan. It was about training, understanding, getting better — and passing this art on.

Today, many years later, what I feel most is gratitude. And yes, a little pride — not because everything was perfect, but because something real grew out of something small. A hobby became a calling. An idea became a school. And students slowly became a kind of family — people who share the same passion and push each other forward.

And even that is temporary — not in the sense of "it will end," but in the sense that it changes. A calling rarely stays exactly the same. It grows, it becomes quieter or bigger, but it stays alive.

I've been teaching since 1995. A lot has changed, but what matters stayed: the joy of teaching, the glow in someone's face when they suddenly understand something, and that special energy inside a good training session.

Maybe you, dear reader, ask yourself this exact question: how do you find your calling and the courage to do what you love — through highs and lows?

Before I answer that, I want to share an old Chinese saying:

"If you want to be happy for an hour, take a nap.
If you want to be happy for a day, go fishing.

If you want to be happy for a year, inherit a fortune. If you want to be happy for a lifetime, help others." — Chinese proverb

You've read this far and you know me a bit now. People like to say, "Money isn't everything." And when you combine that with the thought that in the end everything is only borrowed anyway, the direction becomes clear.

Helping others means more. It's priceless — and it lasts. Because the people you help don't just feel happy. They grow. And that's the beautiful thing about helping: you leave footprints. Real impressions. Something money can't buy.

For me, Wing Chun started as a hobby — pure passion. Over the years more people wanted to train. It grew, became more intense, and then came the moment where I had to make a decision.

At that time I was self employed in sales, out in the field. I'll talk more about that chapter in Volume 2 of this series, but what matters here is this: both together didn't work anymore. The day wasn't long enough.

In the year 2000 I stood in front of a choice: continue a well paid job with unusually good opportunities — or fully focus on the martial arts school, with much lower expectations for income.

You already know what I chose. And I never regretted it.

About courage, I asked myself something simple:

What's the worst that can happen?

Courage doesn't mean you feel no fear. Courage means you move anyway, because you know:

Fear is temporary too.

It doesn't stay.

But what you build can stay.

Of course there was responsibility — rent, private costs, business costs. Everything had to work. But if it hadn't been enough, I would have taken extra jobs or found other income streams. Because anyone who truly wants to work can find work.

And yes, the truth is: for one or two years I really did have to earn extra money to keep the school stable. It was hard. Today I know: hard times always feel like "forever," but they aren't. They're a phase. And that understanding carried me through many days.

But seeing those happy faces every day, feeling the bond between kids, teens, and adults — that sense that something is growing here that truly helps people — it was worth the effort.

And besides… quitting was never my thing.

With a team that feels like a second family, we've now won over 40 world titles. Seeing students apply what we built together at tournaments is a powerful feeling — not because of medals, but because it proves something:

Training works. Work is worth it. People grow.

Success is not an accident. Behind it is discipline, trust, connection — and a lot of repetition, even on days when you don't feel like it.

It's a gift to be allowed to do what you love. Many people work for years in jobs that don't fulfill them. They dream, but they never take the step. Here, that luck was there — and it creates real appreciation.

In recent years something else came into my life: writing. At first it was small notes, thoughts, sentences. Then it grew — not as a replacement, but as an addition. Another way to share what moves you.

Teaching still comes first. But writing helps me sort things out, reflect, and sometimes let go.

When you look back, you don't only see wins. You also see setbacks, detours, hard seasons — and those often shaped you the most.

And while these lines are being written, one thing becomes clear again:

Even this time — as beautiful as it is right now — will one day be a memory.

Everything is temporary.

And maybe that is the greatest gift.

The Next Chapter

A while ago, someone asked me, "When is a book like this actually finished?"

I smiled, because it sounds like an easy question. But it isn't. Because when is anything ever truly finished? A house. A relationship. A season of life. Even a thought.

The most honest answer is often: never completely.

Because everything changes. Because we change. Because life keeps giving us new angles to look from. That's why this sentence fits here too:

Everything is temporary. Even the feeling of "finished."

While I was writing the final lines, I realized something. An ending is rarely a real ending. It's more like a pause. A place to look back for a second, take a breath, and let things sink in.

More than once I thought, "This is the last chapter." And then something else showed up. A memory. A conversation. A moment. And suddenly there was one more topic that belonged here too.

At some point, you still have to decide: for this moment, it's complete. Not because there isn't more to say, but because it's time to take a break. Because just like in life, writing also needs space to breathe.

For me, this book is not something you close and put away like a finished product. It's more like a conversation. Between me and you.

Maybe while reading, you thought of your own experiences. Maybe something came back to you that had been buried for a long time. Maybe a thought rose up that you would like to share.

That's exactly what I hope for. That the book doesn't stop at the final line, but continues inside you.

So here is my invitation:

If you've lived a story that fits this theme, something that showed you how quickly life can change, or a moment that moved you deeply, write to me. It can be just a few bullet points. A short story. Or one simple thought.

Out of messages like that, Volume 2 can grow. A collection of real moments. From real life. From people like you.

I would read the submissions, select some, and shape them into new chapters, the same way I did here. And if you want, your name can be mentioned in the next book. Not as a big headline. Just as a sign that words connect, and that thoughts can be carried forward.

Because this book is not only my project. It's also a piece of shared life, passed on through words, experiences, and feelings.

We all carry stories that can help others see life a little lighter. Sometimes it's something small. A sentence. A look. A meeting. And suddenly something shifts inside.

A story that touched me deeply came from my younger brother:

A father was always busy, always mentally at work. A little boy walked up to him and asked, "Dad, how much do you make per hour?" The father felt interrupted and answered quickly, "20 euros."

The boy walked away. Later he came back and asked softly, "Dad, can you lend me 10 euros?" The father got impatient. "What do you need that for? You just got allowance."

The boy said, "I still have my 10 euros. If you lend me 10 more, I'll have 20." The father didn't understand where this was going.

Then the boy said, "Then I can buy one hour of your time."

That sentence stays with you. It's so simple. And it shows what matters in the end.

If you want to send me your thoughts, ideas, or short experiences, you can do it by email:

book@ml-publishing.com

Maybe you will find yourself in the next book, in a chapter inspired by your life. Because this book doesn't truly end here. It continues. In you. In me. In all the stories that still want to be told.

And the best part is this: we remind each other what really counts.

Even this ending is only temporary.

Sometimes Longer, Sometimes Shorter

Sometimes it helps to stop seeing life as one huge block, and start seeing it as many smaller seasons.

If we're honest, our lives are made of transitions. From one phase to the next. Sometimes smooth. Sometimes hard. Sometimes planned. Sometimes sudden. But in the end, it's always a change.

Birth. Kindergarten. Elementary school. The next school. Vocational training or college. First job. Second job. Maybe a new qualification. Further training. New coworkers. New rules. New worries. New chances.

And it's the same in private life. First relationship. Second relationship. Maybe a breakup. Maybe a fresh start. Maybe the great love. Maybe a detour that hurts, but makes you stronger.

And then there are the seasons nobody wants, but they still come. Illness. Surgery. Real fear. Or simply the moment you realize: health is not guaranteed.

First apartment. Second apartment. A move. A new home. New neighbors. New routes. And also the good things. First vacation. Second vacation. New places. New memories.

When you look at it like that, one thing becomes clear: none of it lasts forever. Some things last weeks. Some stretch over years. But even years will end. And later, when you look back, you often realize: that was "just" a season.

I believe this is one of the most important truths in life.

Because when you're inside a season, it often feels like it will never end, whether it's beautiful or painful. You want to hold on to the good. You want to get rid of the hard right away. But neither really works.

The good doesn't last forever. And the hard can feel like forever. But it passes too. Both are temporary.

And I don't mean that in a cold way. I mean it as comfort. Because it gives you air.

If you're in a difficult time right now, remember this: it's a season, not your whole life.

And if you're in a good time right now, remember this too: it's also a season. Enjoy it. Be here. Be present. Because the good also moves on.

Many people live as if everything is final. A fight becomes a disaster. A mistake becomes the end of the world. Bad news becomes fear for the entire future.

But we all know the truth: we've already survived so much.

When I look at my own life, I see exactly that. There were times I thought, "I can't take this." Today they are memories. And there were moments so beautiful I wanted to freeze them. Today they are warm pictures in my mind. Everything kept moving. Season by season.

Maybe that's a good way to look at life. Not to make it smaller, but to make it lighter.

Because it creates less pressure. You don't have to control everything. You can't hold everything. You can't prevent everything. But you can live consciously.

You can ask yourself more often: What season am I in right now? What matters right now? What helps me? What doesn't? What can I change, and what can't I?

And sometimes one sentence is enough to calm you down:

It’s only a chapter.

When you look at your past, you almost always see it. Whether it was a good time or a hard time, in the end it was “only” a season. Sometimes longer, sometimes shorter, but not your whole life.

And that’s exactly why it’s worth taking the moment seriously, but not too heavily.

Because this moment is temporary too.

Partnership

I only speak about my wife Silvina in detail now, and there's a reason for that.

Everything I wrote about before lies in the past. Thoughts, experiences, memories, moments that passed. A blink in eternity.

With Silvina, it's different. This isn't a look back. It isn't an old story. This is now. While these lines are being written, it's alive. It breathes. It exists.

That's why I didn't want to place it somewhere between other chapters. It stands on its own here at the end, as what remains.

And maybe that already says a lot.

It's no coincidence that I saved her in my phone as "La Mujer de mi Vida" "the woman of my life." For me, that name is not just romance. It means arriving. Calm. That feeling that something finally fits.

A real partnership doesn't show itself on the easy days. It shows itself when life tests you.

Silvina came into my life when a lot was already behind me. I had carried many things. And I had spent years alone with my youngest child. For ten years I was father and mother at the same time.

Then she was there.

And suddenly there was a person who didn't just see me, but also my child.

When the outing happened, it wasn't an easy road. But Silvina stood with us from the beginning. Without hesitation. Without conditions. With an open heart and real understanding. No pressure. No "why." Just there. With love. With calm. With strength.

From 2021 on, she supported us wherever she could. And she often carried me when I had to stay strong. She gave me the calm I needed to write again.

Years before we met, I had started working on *The Art of Wing Chun.* But I didn't truly move forward, because I was missing something very simple: peace.

With her, that changed. She created space for my thoughts. She let me work in silence. And she understood that creativity needs time. No pushing. No complaining. Just a quiet "go."

But our partnership wasn't only words.

There was also sweat and dust.

Together we bought a 120 year old house that had to be fully renovated. Nine months of work. No weekends. No holidays. No Christmas. While others enjoyed their free time, we stood in dust. Paint on our hands. Sore muscles in our arms.

We did around 90 percent ourselves. Plastering, filling, painting, laying floors, building walls. Often late into the night. And Silvina didn't fall behind for a second. She worked where others would have quit long ago.

That time was hard. But like everything in life, it was temporary.

Today we live in a warm, cozy home. And every wall, every floor carries our shared work inside it. That feels like arriving.

For me, that is real partnership. Not big words. But action. Not love only when it's easy, but staying close when it gets hard.

And if you, like me, have gone through relationships or marriages that didn't work out, don't stop looking. I want to believe that there is someone for everyone. A person who loves you, balances you, grows with you, builds something with you.

Not perfect. But right.

Not loud. But real.

Maybe you're thinking, dear reader: "Wait, and with Silvina it isn't temporary? I thought everything is temporary."

And the answer is: of course it's temporary too. Like everything.

It's just this: if life continues as it has, then one of us would have to leave this world before we can look back and say, "That was temporary."

And hopefully that is still decades away.

Until then, for me it's simply what counts: being together, holding each other, keeping going, laughing together, living together as well as we can for as long as we can.

I'm grateful that Silvina is part of my life. Not because she always made it easier, but because she made it more real.

Thank you, Silvina. For your calm. For your strength. And for everything that can't truly be put into words.

Final Thought

When I look back on my life, I see joy and pain, wins and losses, love and goodbyes. Like a path that goes up and down. But more than anything, I see movement.

Nothing stayed the way it was. And in hindsight, that was often a good thing.

Over time, I've learned to take life a little less heavily. To get less worked up about things I can't change. And to enjoy more consciously what's right in front of me.

We are all part of this big current called life. Sometimes calm. Sometimes stormy. But always moving. We can't stop it. We can only learn to move with it.

And if we're honest, it's not the big milestones that matter most in the end. It's the small moments. A look. A laugh. A sentence at the right time. Someone who shows up. A hand on the shoulder. A quiet second where you realize: this is enough.

Maybe that's the real strength: not needing to control everything, not having to fight every battle, but knowing when it's time to let go.

And that's the essence of this book, and maybe of life itself:

Don't take it so hard. Enjoy more. Stay in the present more often. Because this moment is temporary too.

Because everything is temporary.

Preview of Volume 2

Volume 2 is in the works. These are early working titles. Some things may change, but the direction feels right.

- Suzi the Duck
- Marbles
- Social Connections
- The Needle
- Will You Go Out With Me?
- Kings of Death
- Fratellini
- The '80s
- The Trigger That Started It: Wing Chun
- Jennifer Lopez
- Meatball Betty
- Suddenly a Stepfather
- Field Sales
- Stepfather II

Acknowledgements

No one writes a book completely alone.

Even when many hours at the desk feel quiet and solitary, a book is always shaped by encounters, conversations, memories, and by the people we meet along the way.

Thank you, Silvina, *mi amor.* For your patience, your understanding, and your love.

You carried me through phases when I doubted myself. You gave me calm when I needed it. And you were there without pushing, without conditions, simply there.

And because you read so much, almost never seen in the evening without a book, you were able to give me your perspective as a reader again. That helped me make this book more enjoyable to read, clearer and smoother, more human.

Thank you to my children.

Through you, I learned so much about patience, responsibility, and what truly matters in life. Many thoughts in this book were born from moments I lived with you. You were, and still are, my inspiration.

Thank you to my friends, my students, and to everyone who walked along the path with me, and to every reader.

For conversations, questions, the encouragement, and sometimes even the challenges. Every encounter left traces, and many of those traces live in this book.

A special thank you goes to Mico for the editing and Dr. Ramona Lorenz for the sharp eye for detail. With her scientific precision and calm manner, she truly improved this book.

About the Author

Mario Lopez lives in Duisburg/Germany with his wife, Silvina. He writes the way he lives: direct, honest, and without unnecessary fluff.

When he's not teaching or writing, he's happiest spending time with family and friends, playing pool, or riding his motorcycle. He enjoys the moment and keeps reminding himself of one simple truth:

Everything is temporary.

Recommended Reading

The Explosive Art of Close Range Combat — by Randy Williams Six volumes with applications, techniques, and thoughts on Wing Chun.

Close Range Combat Wing Chun — by Randy Williams Three volumes focused on developing and deepening the Wing Chun system.

My Gift for Your Enjoyable Quit-Smoking Journey — by Peter Kruse (Mein Geschenk für deine genussvolle Raucherentwöhnung) Entertaining, motivating, and never preachy.

The Art of Wing Chun — by Mario Lopez My first book, with over 100 QR codes that link directly to videos. Ideal for beginners, advanced students, and instructors.

Thank You

If you've made it this far, thank you.

Maybe you recognized yourself in some lines. Maybe you thought of someone. Maybe one chapter made you smile or made you go quiet for a moment. That's exactly why I wrote this book.

Not to tell you how to live, but to remind you that life gets lighter when you understand this:

Everything changes.

If you're going through a hard time, I wish you strength and patience. This will pass too. And if you're in a good season, I hope you enjoy it fully in the present — with attention and gratitude — because moments like this turn into memories so quickly.

Take care of yourself. And don't forget, from time to time, to simply be here.

Everything is temporary.

Mario Lopez

www.ingramcontent.com/pod-product-compliance
Lightning Source LLC
LaVergne TN
LVHW051008080826
845145LV00009B/2512

* 9 7 8 3 9 1 2 3 7 3 1 5 8 *